A True Adventure

THE STORY OF
THREE WHALES

WRITTEN BY GILES WHITTELL   *ILLUSTRATED BY PATRICK BENSON*

TELEGRAPH BOOKS / WALKER BOOKS

First published 1988 by Telegraph Books/Walker Books. Text © 1988 Giles Whittell. Illustrations © 1988 Patrick Benson
First printed 1988. Printed and bound by Lawrence Allen Ltd, Weston-Super-Mare, U.K.

British Library Cataloguing in Publication Data
Whittell, Giles The story of three whales. 1. Whales. For children. I.Title. II.Benson, Patrick. 599.5

ISBN 0-7445-1367-7

For twelve bright weeks every summer, the Arctic Ocean is full of life. Blooms of plankton float among the icebergs. Shellfish slide along the sea floor. Squid lurk under pitch-black overhangs of rock. And whales swim up from the Pacific to feed.

Humpback whales, Bowhead whales and California Grey whales all come to the Arctic. In the summer of 1988 one particular herd of California Greys was plunging and rolling, leaping and belly-flopping, off the north coast of Alaska.

But winter came early in 1988. The first sign was a freezing wind from the east. Blizzards blew in from the top of the world. Thick pack-ice spread out from the shore and its shadow fell over the whales.

Most of the whales were quick to sense the changes. In small groups, they set off on the long swim south to warmth for the winter. But three of the whales failed to notice the end of summer – one adult, one middle-sized, one baby.

Quietly the ice crept in. The ocean was changing from blue to silent white. Grey whales can hold their breath under water for half an hour, but soon the three who had been left behind would have nowhere left to surface.

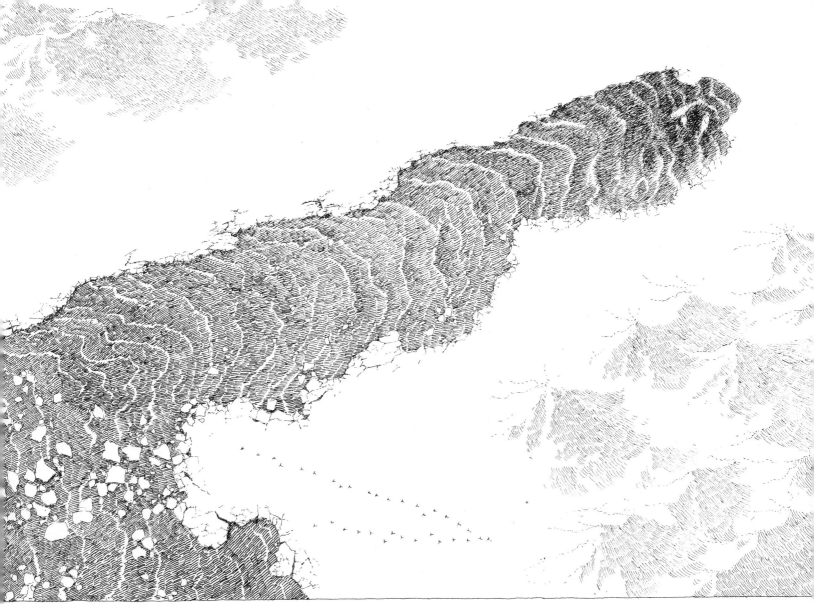

Only the open water was safe, beyond the pack-ice. But the three whales lost their sense of direction. They swam towards land, into an Alaskan bay, where the still, shallow water was certain to freeze very quickly.

At the mouth of the bay was a shelf of ice, under water. Broken pack-ice piled up against it, forming a wall. From sea-bed to surface there was no way out.

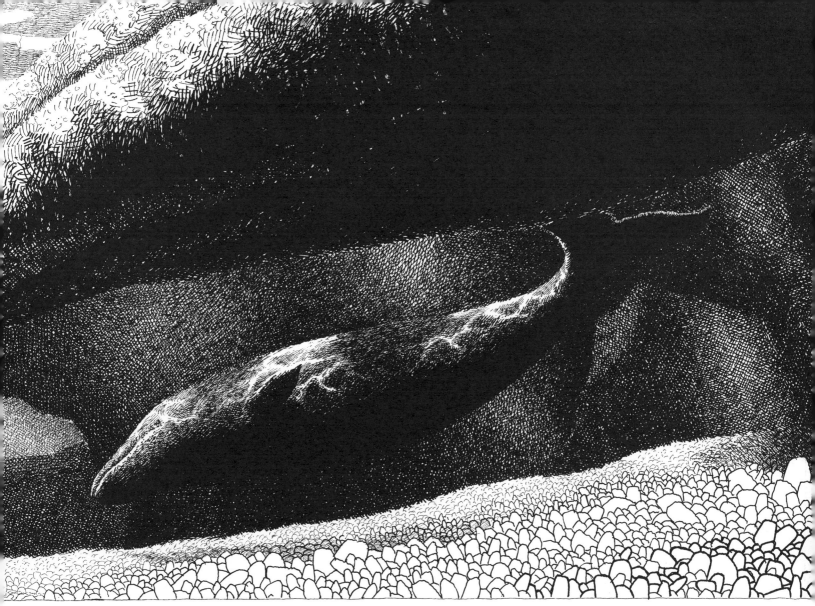

Then the surface froze solid. The whales were trapped in a prison of ice. They could not breathe. Again and again they rammed upwards at the ice with their noses.

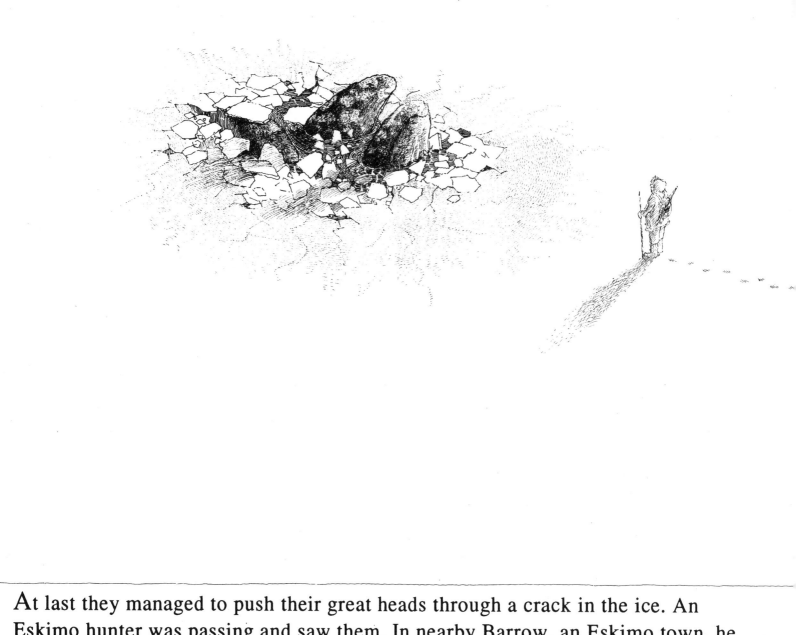

At last they managed to push their great heads through a crack in the ice. An Eskimo hunter was passing and saw them. In nearby Barrow, an Eskimo town, he told people what he had seen.

To begin with nothing was done to save the whales. It would be natural for the whales to die and the Eskimos accepted it. But the news of the whales began to spread. Their pictures appeared on local TV.

One person who heard the news was a wildlife ranger. She persuaded the people of Barrow to help keep the whales alive. Out over the ice they trudged, with axes, ice-poles and chainsaws to cut breathing holes.

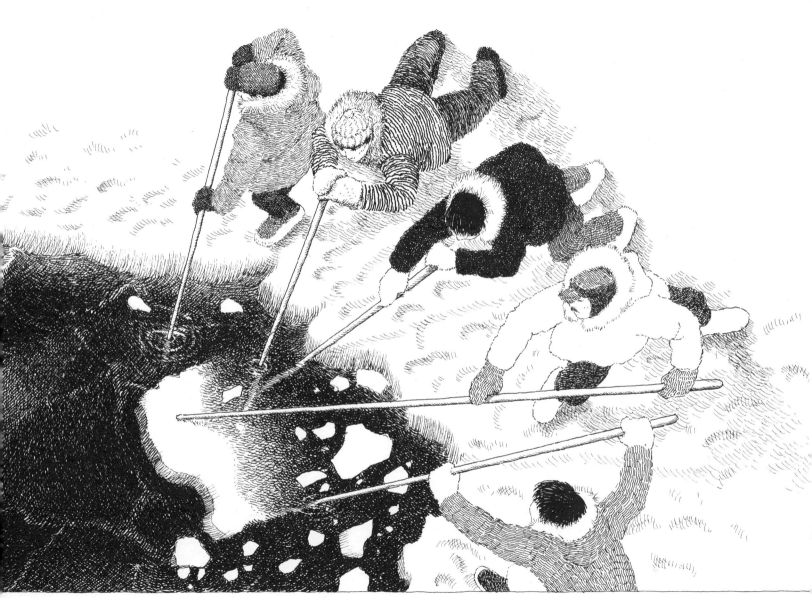

The whales appeared at the holes and filled their huge lungs. The Eskimos gave them names: Siku (the biggest), Poutu (the middle one) and Kannick (the baby). *Siku* means ice in Eskimo. *Poutu* means ice-hole and *Kannick* means snowflake.

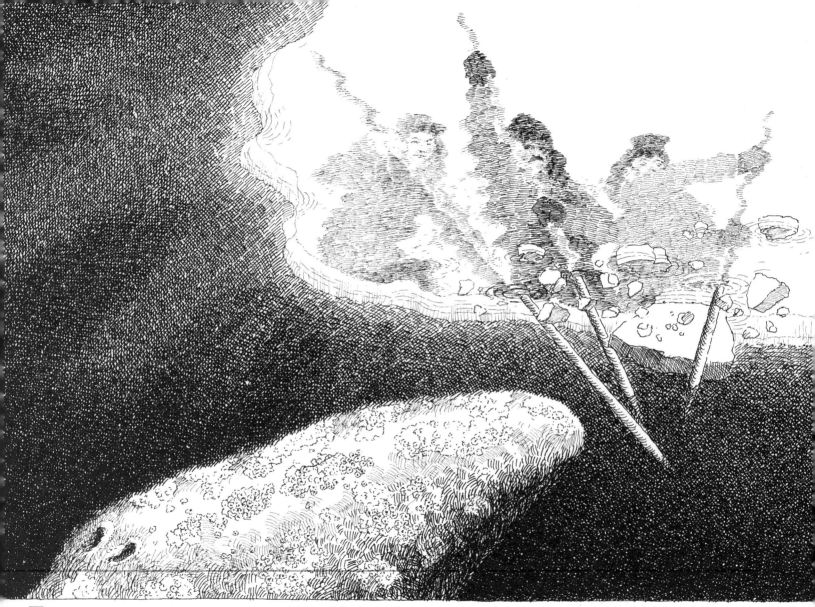

The Eskimos cut a line of breathing holes, out towards the open water. They worked for fourteen days and nights. Clattering chainsaws sliced constantly through the ice, but the water would quickly freeze solid again.

Siku, Poutu and Kannick refused to follow the line of holes. They stayed by the shore where they knew they could breathe. "The Plight of the Whales" became front-page news all over the world. Millions of people waited in hope.

From all across America, offers of help poured in. But nothing could break through the wall of ice at the mouth of the bay. An enormous bulldozer tried, but stuck fast.

A sky-crane helicopter hammered the ice with a concrete torpedo. It punched a line of holes from the whales to the wall. But still the whales wouldn't follow.

Their noses were bloody and scraped to the bone. The ice was invincible. It seemed to the watching world that the whales must die. Polar bears stalked the ice, waiting patiently for a feast of whale-meat.

One evening Siku and Poutu surfaced alone. Being the smallest, Kannick was also the weakest. Morning came and still only Siku and Poutu appeared at the hole. No one could say exactly what had happened. And no one ever saw Kannick again.

On the twentieth day, Siku and Poutu felt the tremble of distant engines. A huge Russian ice-breaker was roaring to the rescue, the great *Admiral Makarov*.

The captain found a grand phrase to mark the occasion. "Let us begin to break ice!" he called. All night the breaker charged at the ice, pulled back, and charged again.

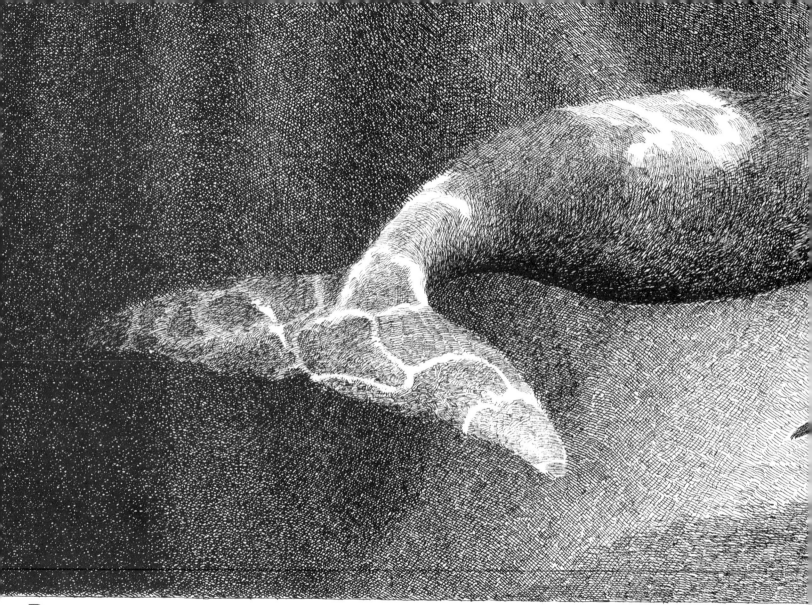

By morning a channel was clear, a quarter of a mile wide. The crew of the *Admiral Makarov* grinned. They came ashore to celebrate and the Eskimos and other Americans hugged them and cheered.

Then the ice-breaker turned for the open sea with Siku and Poutu close behind. The whales understood that they must follow the thunder and froth of the engines. The sound would lead them from the prison of ice, to the open water and freedom.

The rest of the herd was three weeks ahead on the journey south. Siku and Poutu had thousands of miles to swim. So they each blew a great waterspout and set off. Their long ordeal was over now.